"I used to walk down the street like I was a star... I want people to walk around delusional about how great they can be - and then to fight so hard for it every day that the lie becomes the truth"
Fold Back
DOLL 1

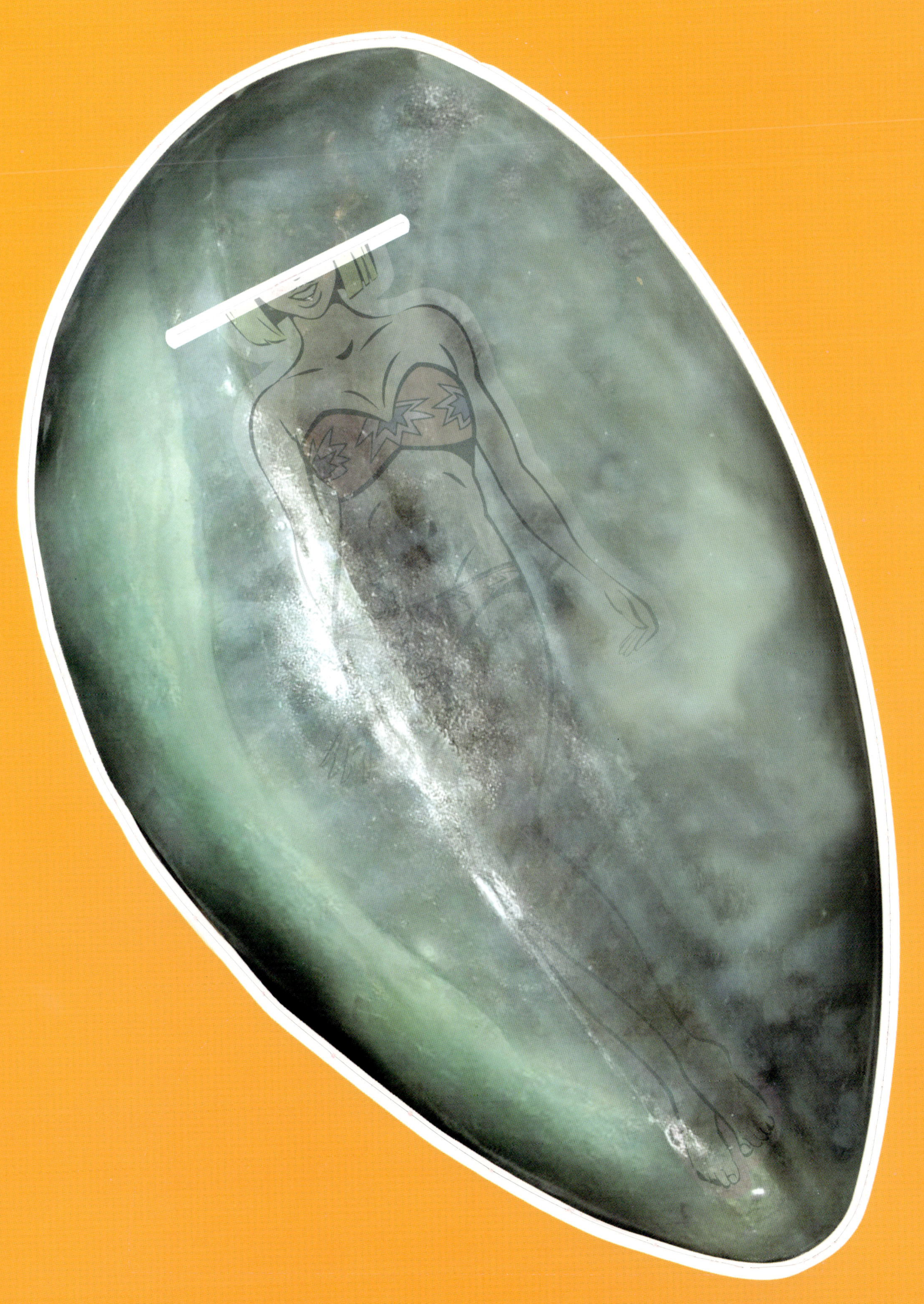

DOLL 1
DOLL 1
DOLL 1
DOLL 1

DOLL 1
DOLL 1

DOLL 1

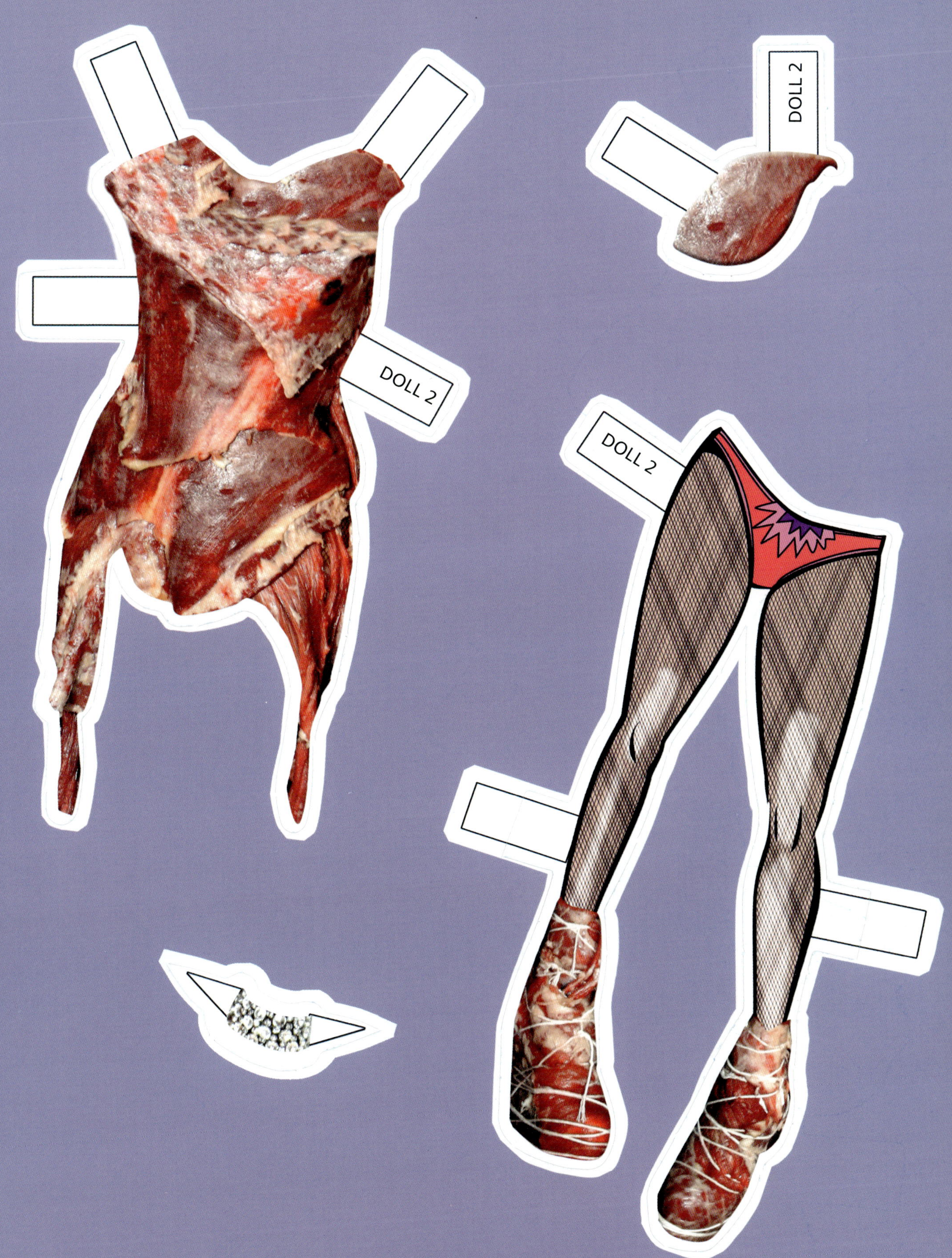
DOLL 2
DOLL 2
DOLL 2

DOLL 2
DOLL 2

DOLL 2
Fold Back to stand
Fold Back to stand
Fold Back to stand

DOLL 2
DOLL 2
DOLL 2

DOLL 2
DOLL 2

DOLL 2
DOLL 2

DOLL 2
DOLL 1
DOLL 2
DOLL 1
DOLL 1

DOLL 1
DOLL 1
DOLL 2
DOLL 1

DOLL 1
DOLL 2
DOLL 2

DOLL 1

DOLL 2

DOLL 2

Fold Back to stand

THIS IS A CARLTON BOOK

Published in 2011 by Carlton Books Limited
20 Mortimer Street
London W1T 3JW

10 9 8 7 6 5 4 3

A CIP catalogue record for this book is available from the British Library.

ISBN 978 1 84732 942 4

Printed in China

Senior Executive Editor: Lisa Dyer
Managing Art Editor: Lucy Coley
Design: A&E
Picture Research: Jenny Meredith
Production: Maria Petalidou

ACKNOWLEDGEMENTS
The publishers would like to thank the following sources for their kind permission to reproduce the pictures in this book.
Key, t: top, b: bottom, l: left, r: right.

Rex Features: 3bl, 5r, 19, 21br, 23bl, 31, /Action Press: 21tr, 25tr, 25br, /Matt Baron/BEI: 9, /Billy Farrell Agency: 3tl, 3br, /Mark Campbell: 23tl, /Copetti/Photofab/MCP: 21tl, /David Fisher: 11; 13, /Henry Lamb/BEI: 21bl, 25bl, /NBCUPHOTOBANK: 29, /Picture Perfect: 7, /Brian Rasic: 19, /Brian J. Ritchie/Hotsauce: 21c, /Sipa Press: 1, 23tr, 25tl, 25b, /Startraks Photo: 5l, 25tr, /Dennis Stone: 15, /Richard Young: 17,

Every effort has been made to acknowledge correctly and contact the source and/or copyright holder of each picture and Carlton Books Limited apologizes for any unintentional errors or omissions which will be corrected in future editions of this book.

Quote on insert Doll 1:
Poker Face: The Rise and Rise of Lady Gaga, Maureen Callahan, Hyperion, 2010.

Quote on insert Doll 2:
'Lady Gaga, Adele, Rihanna: Only Girls Allowed,' *The Telegraph*, Neil McCormick, 1 June 2011.

"Some women choose to follow men, and some women choose to follow their dreams. If you're wondering which way to go, remember that your career will never wake up and tell you that it doesn't love you anymore"
Fold Back
DOLL 2